SPECIAL REPORTS

FRACKING

BY KATHRYN HULICK

CONTENT CONSULTANT

ANTHONY J. MARCHESE, PhD
PROFESSOR OF MECHANICAL ENGINEERING
COLORADO STATE UNIVERSITY

Essential Library

An Imprint of Abdo Publishing | abdopublishing.com

abdopublishing.com

Printed in the United States of America, North Mankato, Minnesota
092016
012017

THIS BOOK CONTAINS RECYCLED MATERIALS

Cover Photo: Brennan Linsley/AP Images
Interior Photos: Jim Lo Scalzo/EPA/Newscom, 4–5; Melanie Stetson Freeman/The Christian Science Monitor/Getty Images, 8; Songquan Deng/Shutterstock Images, 13; akg-images/Straube/Newscom, 14–15; Pat Sullivan/AP Images, 17, 75; iStockphoto, 21; Robert Ingelhart/iStockphoto, 24–25; Adrian Wyld/The Canadian Press/AP Images, 29; Nigel Cattlin/Alamy, 31; Paul Hellstern/The Oklahoman/AP Images, 34–35; Mike Groll/AP Images, 38; Charles Rex Arbogast/AP Images, 42; Christopher Boswell/Shutterstock Images, 44; John Gomez/Shutterstock Images, 45; Romiana Lee/Shutterstock Images, 46–47; Damian Dovarganes/AP Images, 53; Ringo Chiu/ZumaPress/Newscom, 55; Matthew Brown/AP Images, 57; L. M. Otero/AP Images, 58–59; Shutterstock Images, 61, 79, 92–93; Alex Milan Tracy/Sipa/AP Images, 63; J. B. Nicholas/Splash News/Newscom, 68–69; Keith Srakocic/AP Images, 80–81; Sue Ogrocki/AP Images, 83; Julie Dermansky/Science Source, 91; Jeff Chiu/AP Images, 96

Editor: Mirella Miller
Series Designer: Maggie Villaume

Publisher's Cataloging-in-Publication Data

Names: Hulick, Kathryn, author.
Title: Fracking / by Kathryn Hulick.
Description: Minneapolis, MN : Abdo Publishing, 2017. | Series: Special reports |
      Includes bibliographical references and index.
Identifiers: LCCN 2016945212 | ISBN 9781680783933 (lib. bdg.) |
      ISBN 9781680797466 (ebook)
Subjects: LCSH: Hydraulic fracturing--Juvenile literature.
Classification: DDC 622/.3381--dc23
LC record available at http://lccn.loc.gov/2016945212

CONTENTS

CHAPTER ONE

FLAMING
TAP WATER

S herry Vargson turned on the water in her kitchen. She struck a match and then held it by the stream of water. Foom! A small fireball erupted from the faucet. It was 2011, and she had been having problems with her water for a year. In the winter, her horse's outdoor trough of water did not freeze, even when temperatures dropped to –14 degrees Fahrenheit (–26°C). Vargson believed her water contained high levels of methane, an extremely flammable gas.

Vargson blamed hydraulic fracturing, or fracking, for the problems. This technique injects a mixture of water, sand, and chemicals into the ground at high pressure in order to release natural gas and other fossil fuels from deep underground rock formations. The process

Sherry Vargson lights her sink water on fire, showing that methane has leaked into her home's well.

of drilling for and extracting fuel from rock formations involves many steps besides fracking. But most people use the term to refer to the entire process. Natural gas, which is made up of methane and other gases, is a valuable natural resource used to generate electricity, manufacture chemicals, and more.

WHAT'S IN A NAME?

The word *fracking* is catchy and easy to remember. For that reason, activists plaster it across protest signs. From the gas industry's point of view, though, fracking refers only to a relatively short step in the natural gas production process. This step involves cracking apart rocks deep underground. When opponents argue that fracking contaminates water or threatens people's health, the industry often counters that these claims are false. But in 2016, former EPA scientist Dominic DiGiulio proved that fracking fluid had contaminated groundwater in Wyoming. Other aspects of the process of drilling for gas may be more problematic. In addition, not all drilling operations use fracking to prepare a well. Using the word *fracking* to refer to the entire process of drilling for, extracting, and transporting fossil fuels leads to many misunderstandings.

In 2007, Vargson agreed to let a local company, Chesapeake Energy, drill a well for natural gas on her property in Granville Township, Pennsylvania. The company paid her for the use of her land. "The land man told us they would come in, they would drill, they would frack, they would reclaim [clean up] the area, and leave us within a very short time frame," she said.[1] Instead, her life changed when her water supply became contaminated.

NATURAL OR NOT?

Vargson claimed the contamination happened after Chesapeake Energy performed maintenance at the well on her property in June 2010. Two days later, Vargson noticed her faucet was sputtering a lot. A representative from the company tested her water and found methane levels far above the danger level. To control the problem, the company installed a vent pipe at the water well to help release excess gas. Methane is not poisonous, but it can detonate when exposed to a spark or a flame. Other Pennsylvania residents living near gas wells had experienced fires and explosions as a result of methane-contaminated drinking water wells.

FOSSIL FUELS

Fossil fuels, including coal, petroleum, and natural gas, come from the remains of ancient animals and plants that lived during the Carboniferous period approximately 286 to 360 million years ago. After these animals and plants died, they were buried under layers of earth, sand, and clay. Heat and pressure slowly transformed them into fossil fuels. Coal looks like a black or brown rock. Petroleum, also called crude oil, is a black, gooey substance. Factories refine petroleum into many products, including gasoline. The gas in a car, however, is very different from natural gas. Natural gas, which is composed mostly of methane, is invisible, lighter than air, and typically odorless. All of these fossil fuels contain energy in the form of carbon and hydrogen. Burning coal, oil, or gas produces power that people use for transportation, electricity, and more.

In addition, when methane leaks into the air, it contributes to climate change.

Methane in a water well does not necessarily come from gas drilling operations, however. Northern Pennsylvania, where Vargson lives, contains a lot of natural gas beneath the ground. Even before companies drilled and fracked for gas in the area, some people had contaminated water. When faced with complaints from people such as Vargson, gas companies often claim the contamination is natural. This may be true in some cases, but improperly drilled natural gas wells can leak. Those leaks may contaminate water.

A 2013 study by researchers at Duke University tested the water at 141 homes in northeastern Pennsylvania. They found methane in 82 percent of those water wells. The water wells within 0.6 miles (1 km) of a natural gas drilling operation contained six times more methane than average. The study concluded that drilling

"I BELIEVE THAT WE ARE DOING EVERYTHING WE CAN TO CONSTRUCT OUR WELLS PROPERLY AND SAFELY AND THAT WE ARE NOT CONTRIBUTING TO THE PROBLEM."[2]

—DAVID BERT, VICE PRESIDENT OF DRILLING, CHESAPEAKE ENERGY

Vargson points out the vent that Chesapeake Energy installed on her land to reduce the methane levels in her farm's water.

operations had contaminated the water. In May 2011, the Pennsylvania Department of Environmental Protection (DEP) ordered Chesapeake Energy to pay a $900,000 fine for contaminating the drinking water at 16 homes, including Vargson's. "It sounds like the state is going to get a chunk of change. But I still have contaminated water," said Vargson.[3]

A FRACKING MESS

In Dimock Township, Pennsylvania, residents have also complained about water contamination due to drilling by Cabot Oil & Gas. Some of the contamination may be natural. The town, however, has attracted a media frenzy, partially due to the 2010 documentary film *Gasland*, which painted an unpleasant picture of a town poisoned by gas drilling. The film fed a growing anti-fracking movement, even though many of the stories in the film are unreliable and not backed up by scientific evidence. The issue has split Dimock down the middle. One group blames fracking

"MOST OF US BELIEVE METHANE IS THE LEAST OF OUR WORRIES. WE'LL NEVER DRINK OUR WATER."[4]

—VICTORIA SWITZER, RESIDENT OF DIMOCK, PENNSYLVANIA

MORE TO THE
STORY

WELCOME TO DIMOCK, PENNSYLVANIA

On January 1, 2009, Norma Fiorentino's well exploded. She was not home at the time, but the blast broke an eight-foot- (2.4 m) wide concrete slab into pieces and rained them onto her lawn. After the explosion, she and other residents of Dimock worried about the safety of their water. Cabot Oil & Gas had recently started drilling for natural gas in the area. Fifteen families sued Cabot. The company claimed the methane contamination happened naturally. But the Pennsylvania Department of Environmental Protection (DEP) disagreed. The DEP ordered the company to stop all drilling activity, pay a fine of $120,000, and pay for a pipeline to bring clean water to residents.

In 2012, the Environmental Protection Agency (EPA) reported finding toxic chemicals in the water at five homes, but treatment systems could make the water safe. "The sampling and an evaluation of the particular circumstances at each home did not indicate levels of contaminants that would give EPA reason to take further action," said regional administrator Shawn Garvin.[5] In 2012, the DEP also lifted its suspension on drilling in the area.

Meanwhile, the town of Dimock became ground zero for the fracking debate. The issue has pitted neighbor against neighbor. Some still refuse to drink their water. Others say the water is fine, and that antifracking activists are blowing things out of proportion.

for health problems ranging from dizziness to skin sores. The other side claims the water is fine and argues fracking boosts the economy.

The controversy goes beyond Dimock. The debate has played out on a national and global scale as well. Environmentalists, liberal citizens, and even celebrities have banded together to oppose fracking. They claim the process of drilling for natural gas pollutes the environment, contributes to global warming, contaminates water, causes earthquakes, and damages the health of people and animals.

Meanwhile, people in the energy business, along with citizens and lawmakers with more conservative views, tend to support fracking. Their arguments note that natural gas drilling spurs industry, creates jobs, and will bring energy independence to the United States. In addition, they claim natural gas is a clean fuel that helps reduce the dangers of climate change. They also say many of their opponents' claims about fracking are either wrong or greatly exaggerated. Moreover, all citizens of the United States,

Natural gas generates a large portion of the country's electricity, heats people's homes, and provides energy for manufactured goods.

liberal and conservative alike, benefit from natural gas production. Whether they like it or not, Americans depend on fracking to get the energy they use every day.

CHAPTER TWO

TRAPPED
IN STONE

I n the 1980s, the United States was running low

on oil and gas. As a result, large companies, such

as ExxonMobil and Chevron, started moving their

operations away from the United States. But Mitchell

Energy, a small drilling company located in Texas,

stuck around.

At the time, most drillers bored a hole straight into

the ground to tap into oil and gas pockets that had

formed in layers of rock such as sandstone. These were

the easiest and cheapest places to drill. Everyone knew

that natural gas and oil could be found in other rock

formations as well. But these reserves were too difficult

or expensive to extract. Shale rocks, especially, trapped

huge reserves of oil and gas.

Workers drill for natural gas in Germany.

In the past, choosing the right spot to drill an oil well meant searching for natural seeps or leaks of oil. Then, in the 1920s, the oil and gas industry started using sound waves to sense beneath solid ground. The process is called seismic imaging. Over the decades, the process has improved dramatically.

Today, a survey team embeds a group of receivers called geophones in the ground. Then they use heavy equipment to hammer on the ground. The vibrations bounce off layers of rock. The vibrations change based on the type of rock they encounter. The geophones collect the reflected vibrations, and a computer analyzes the information to draw detailed, three-dimensional maps of underground formations. These maps tell an energy company exactly where to place a well in order to get the most oil or gas. Thanks to these techniques, the odds of drilling a successful well have increased from 10 percent to more than 50 percent.[1]

Shale began as prehistoric mud. Often, this mud contained the remains of tiny plants and animals. Over time, heat and pressure underground transformed the mud into shale and the organic matter into bits of oil or gas. The amount of heat determined which fossil fuel was produced. These bubbles of oil and gas often remained trapped inside the shale, similar to chocolate chips inside a cookie.

Shale gas was a tempting resource, but it was too expensive and difficult to extract. In fact, many companies would drill right through shale rock formations to get to deeper sandstone deposits. But Mitchell Energy was running out of easy-to-reach gas in the Texas area. George Mitchell decided to drill for shale gas despite the extra expense and risk. Others at the company, including his own son, said Mitchell was wasting his time. "I had no choice, really," Mitchell said. "We had to get the gas to flow."[2]

"THE [MAJOR COMPANIES] DIDN'T BOTHER WITH FRACKING, THEY DIDN'T WANT TO FOOL WITH IT. I SAW IT AS THE NEW TECHNOLOGY."[3]

—GEORGE MITCHELL, MITCHELL ENERGY

No one in the energy business used fracking on shale until Mitchell tried it in 1981.

SLICK WATER

Mitchell turned to hydraulic fracturing as a way to get gas out of shale. Fracking was not a new idea. In fact, the idea of breaking rock to get gas or oil to flow more easily had been around since the middle of the 1800s, when some drillers started using explosives inside oil wells. By the middle of the 1900s, engineers were experimenting with hydraulics, or high-pressure liquids.

Mitchell Energy fracked the shale in Texas for years without much success. But in 1997, everything changed. Engineer Nicholas Steinsberger tried a new mixture of fracking fluid, composed mostly of water, sand, and some chemicals, to help the water flow faster. It turned out to be the secret sauce the company needed to succeed. The technique became known as slick-water fracturing. By 2001, Mitchell Energy's production was booming, thanks to the new fluid. Today, slick-water fracturing is the mainstay of all gas fracking operations.

DRILLING SIDEWAYS

Slick-water fracking alone was not enough to solve the United States' energy problems, though. A second technological breakthrough, called horizontal drilling, helped usher in a new era for energy in the United States.

Shale formations below the ground stretch thin and wide. Traditional drilling goes straight down. To reach more pockets of gas, you need more wells. But each new well is expensive. Starting in the 1970s, engineers working mainly for the US government developed and perfected a technique called horizontal drilling. They could drill straight down to oil- or gas-rich rock, and then turn the drill bit sideways and keep going through the best part of the rock. Without horizontal drilling, a well would typically be able to access 100 feet (30 m) of oil-rich rock. But with the new technology, the well could extend more than one mile (1.6 km). Also, one vertical well could host multiple horizontal arms snaking through the underground shale. In addition, the cracks produced during fracking became more effective in a horizontal well because of the structure of the rock formation.

DIAMOND DRILLING

Before fracking can begin, drillers must cut a hole through solid rock. Shale is an especially tough rock to drill through. US government research led to the development of a diamond-studded drill bit. Diamond is the hardest material on Earth, making it a great cutting tool. The diamonds used for drill bits are produced in labs.

FROM THE
HEADLINES

A BIG SECRET

"This is the biggest secret in the history of the company," said George Mitchell. "No one can hear about this!"[4] It was 1999, and he realized his company, Mitchell Energy, was sitting on a gold mine: the Barnett shale formation in Texas. One of his engineers, Nicholas Steinsberger, had invented a slick-water fracturing fluid. The watery mixture cracked shale in just the right way to release natural gas.

When Steinsberger first experimented with new fracking recipes, many of his colleagues thought he was crazy. At the time, a thick, gel-like liquid was standard for fracking. Pouring water on shale would make a big mess, critics said. At one point, Steinsberger worried he might lose his job for wasting time and money on his idea. But finally, he tweaked his formula in the right way. His approach created numerous, very tiny fractures in the rock. These cracks allowed gas to flow and keep on flowing. One of Steinsberger's experimental wells started out producing a lot of gas per day, which was not particularly unusual. But after 90 days, the well was still going strong. That is when Steinsberger knew he had made a breakthrough.

Meanwhile, geologist Kent Bowker was studying the Barnett shale. He determined it held much more natural gas than anyone had suspected. Bowker convinced Mitchell to buy the rights to drill on even more land.

By the year 2000, rivals in the energy industry noticed what was happening at Mitchell Energy, and they could not believe it. Steinsberger's discovery spread, but he never received a special bonus for his work.

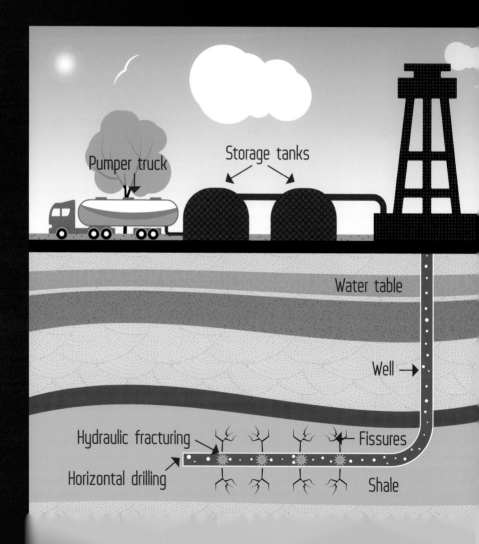

Pumper truck

Storage tanks

Water table

Well →

Hydraulic fracturing — Fissures

Horizontal drilling

Shale

A MIGHTY COMBINATION

Today, a shale gas operation begins with engineers drilling a hole in the ground. The hole can reach as deep as two miles (3.2 km) before they turn the drill sideways to bore through the shale. The engineers add layers of steel and cement casing around the hole to make a solid pipe. The part of the pipe inside the shale contains small holes. Next, the engineers inject fracking fluids at high pressure. The fluid sprays out of the holes into the shale, forming numerous tiny cracks. Finally, the drillers pump the fracking fluid back out of the well. Now, the well is ready for production. The cracks release gas from inside the rock, and the well carries it up to the surface. The fracking process helps prepare a well to be able to extract gas. Fracking lasts up to five days, and the well will produce gas for years or decades.

MORE TO THE
STORY

DRILLS, PUMPS, AND TRUCKS

Getting natural gas or oil out of the ground requires a lot of heavy equipment. A typical drilling site resembles a busy construction site. A drilling rig, which can be the size of a large building, houses all of the equipment necessary to make a hole that extends into the earth. This equipment includes mud tanks, pumps, a huge mast for holding the drill, and power generators.

Trucks of all sizes and shapes carry in the material needed to build and frack the well. Some trucks bring steel pipe to case the well. Others carry sand or chemicals. But for a fracking operation, the most important component is water. It takes 400 to 600 tanker trucks to carry the five million gallons (19 million L) of water necessary to frack one well.[5] After a gas well is complete, large tanks separate fluids from the gas coming out of the well, and noisy compressor stations send the gas into pipelines. From there, it travels to storage facilities or to end users such as power plants.

CHAPTER THREE

FUELING
THE UNITED
STATES

T he United States produces more oil and gas than any other country, contributing 13 percent of the world's oil and 21 percent of its gas.[1] Soon, other countries will buy natural gas from the United States, and the country will likely achieve energy independence. This means drilling, mining, wind farms, solar arrays, and other energy-producing operations located in the United States will provide all of the power needed for US homes, businesses, cars, trucks, airplanes, and more. The International Energy Agency predicts energy independence for the United States by 2035.

Fracked wells currently produce more natural gas than Americans use.

FRIENDS AND ENEMIES

Only ten years ago, energy independence in the United States was unthinkable. Before fracking and horizontal drilling took off, the United States bought oil and gas from foreign countries. Saudi Arabia was the top oil producer, and Russia produced the most natural gas. When a foreign country controls access to energy, political tension can cause big problems. In 1973, and again in 1979, political problems in the Middle East led to oil shortages and high energy prices in the United States. Controlling the oil or gas leads to power and influence.

Buying oil from foreign countries would not be a problem if the countries were friendly neighbors or close allies. But many of the world's most productive oil

OIL CRISIS

In 1973, the United States supported Israel during a conflict in the Middle East. This decision angered Saudi Arabia and other countries in the region. They responded with an oil embargo and stopped exporting oil to the United States and several other countries. This created a shortage of oil in the world, leading to extremely high gasoline prices and long lines at the pumps. A similar situation happened from 1978 through 1979, after a revolution toppled the government of Iran. Oil production in that country plummeted, and global oil markets suffered. Once again, oil prices soared. These two events made it clear that dependence on foreign oil was a big problem for the United States.

fields are in the Middle East, in countries such as Saudi

Arabia, the United Arab Emirates, Iran, and Iraq. Many of

these countries have struggled through instability, wars,

and revolutions. Some have

harbored terrorists or enemies

of the United States. In 2008,

President Barack Obama said,

"One of the most dangerous

weapons in the world today is

the price of oil. We ship nearly

$700 million a day to unstable

or hostile nations for their

oil."[2] This money could end up in the pockets of terrorists

or militants. The United States would prefer not to give

money to its enemies.

> "AFTER YEARS OF TALKING ABOUT IT, WE ARE FINALLY POISED TO CONTROL OUR OWN ENERGY FUTURE. . . . WE PRODUCE MORE NATURAL GAS THAN EVER BEFORE—AND NEARLY EVERYONE'S ENERGY BILL IS LOWER BECAUSE OF IT."[3]
>
> **—PRESIDENT BARACK OBAMA, 2013 STATE OF THE UNION ADDRESS**

Politicians in the United States have talked about the

importance of freedom from foreign oil for years. They

have also introduced and backed policies to help reach

this goal. Some prefer the phrase *energy security* rather

than *energy independence*. This is because a country cannot

be completely disconnected from the global energy

market. The price of oil will always depend on how much

A WAR FOR OIL?

The Iraq War lasted from 2003 through 2011, and through 2016 US troops remained stationed in the country. The reasons for the war were many, including a suspicion that Iraq was building weapons of mass destruction that later proved false. But control over oil fields in the region was one very important factor. Before the war, foreign companies had no access to the oil. The Iraqi government controlled it all. After the conflict, companies such as ExxonMobil and Shell Oil could start drilling there.

is produced around the world. But if the United States makes all of its own energy, a foreign country threatening to shut off access does not matter. The lights will stay on and cars will keep moving thanks to US oil fields. Some journalists have started referring to the United States as "Saudi America," implying this country will remain a global superpower thanks to abundant oil and gas.

THE KEYSTONE XL PIPELINE

Before the fracking boom, the oil industry had operations in Canada mining oil sands. Getting useful fuel out of oil sands requires controversial techniques such as strip mining or heating the oil sands with steam. Even then, the fuel that is produced is of low quality. And these processes produce pollution and release gases that contribute to climate change. But Canada is a friendly neighbor to

Oil sands are thick, gooey deposits of tar mixed with sand, clay, and water.

the United States. These operations could be a more
dependable source of oil than the Middle East.

To move oil from Canada through the United States,
the company TransCanada planned to extend its network
of existing pipelines. Pipelines carry oil from place to
place quickly and efficiently. The Keystone XL Pipeline
project was proposed in 2005 to help transport oil through
Montana, South Dakota, and Nebraska. The project
quickly became the target of environmental protests. In
2015, President Obama rejected the Keystone XL Pipeline
proposal. Obama cited concern for the environment in his
announcement, but fracking was another very important
factor. Companies could now get high-quality oil out of
the ground in North Dakota or Texas. Americans did not

MORE TO THE
STORY

GETTING GAS FROM HERE TO THERE

Transporting natural gas is not simple. If natural gas gets into the air, it spreads out and escapes. It is highly flammable and explosive. The United States relies on a complex system of pipelines to carry gas from place to place. After leaving a well, gas travels to processing plants. These factories remove any liquid fuels that may be mixed in with the gas. Next, pipelines carry gas to power plants or storage facilities. Local distribution networks use trucks to bring natural gas to people's homes for heating and cooking needs.

To push large volumes of gas through pipelines, compressor stations located along the route keep the gas at high pressure. This effectively squashes the gas so it takes up less space and travels more efficiently.

To get to places that do not have pipelines, special facilities can cool natural gas to very low temperatures. This condenses it into a liquid form. Liquid natural gas takes up 600 times less space than regular gas. It can be carried in tanker trucks or ships. Condensing and evaporating natural gas requires special plants that cost billions of dollars to build, but new technology should reduce this cost.

need access to low-quality oil sands in Canada anymore. Many oil sands mining operations have been canceled.

AROUND THE WORLD

The United States and Canada are the only countries in the world where shale oil and gas operations have boomed since the late 2000s. Shale formations rich in gas or oil lie beneath parts of Algeria, Argentina, China, Libya, Mexico, Poland, Russia, and the United Kingdom. China is already investing in shale gas drilling, but it will take a while for any of these countries to catch up to Canada and the

Shale rocks on cliffs in the United Kingdom

United States. Several factors made it easier for fracking to take hold in North America. The area has plenty of freshwater, which fracking requires. North America already had many pipelines and transportation systems needed to move natural gas around. The US government also helped fund research into new energy technologies.

In addition, US laws made it possible for companies to buy the rights to drill on private land. In the United States, a person who buys property typically also buys the rights to the resources located in the ground beneath the property. These resources are called mineral rights. A company that wants the underground resources must pay the property owner for the mineral rights. In some cases, though, drillers use a legal tool

FIRST GAS EXPORT

In 2016, the United States shipped its first export of natural gas overseas. This event marked a reversal in the global energy market. The United States had imported gas for years. In the early 2000s, when natural gas was scarce and expensive, a young energy entrepreneur named Charif Souki invested in import terminals to bring natural gas in from other countries by ship. "Everything was coming along perfectly. But then, of course, 2008 hit, and all of a sudden the genius became the idiot," Souki said.[4] It became clear in 2008 that fracking would make natural gas imports unnecessary. Instead of giving up, Souki decided to turn his import terminals into export terminals. Condensing gas for export was a much more expensive process. But the gamble paid off. His company, Cheniere Energy, is now profitable and building more export terminals.

called forced pooling. This gives them access to minerals beneath private property. In many other countries around the world, the government owns all mineral rights. In the United States, private ownership makes it possible for anyone to seek his or her fortune in the oil and gas business. These entrepreneurs start companies that then compete with each other. This results in many more new wells. In the United States, 4 million oil and gas wells have been drilled, compared to 1.5 million in all other countries combined.[5]

At the beginning of the fracking boom, people and companies who were eager to get rich rushed to buy up mineral rights in areas located over shale formations. Many of these people lived the American dream. They became wealthy through hard work, perseverance, and risk-taking.

HURRICANE KATRINA

In 2005, approximately 20 percent of the natural gas produced in the United States and more than 25 percent of its crude oil came from the Gulf of Mexico.[6] Then Hurricane Katrina swept in and changed everything. More than 1,800 people lost their lives, and millions lost their homes.[7] Thousands of oil and gas wells were also damaged or stopped operating during the storm and its aftermath. As a result, fossil fuel production slowed and prices for oil and gas rose. Over the next few years, though, fracking took off. The Gulf became less important as the country's energy landscape grew to include shale gas and oil. Now, the energy industry no longer fears hurricane damage as much as it used to.

CHAPTER FOUR

BILLIONAIRE
OR BUST

George Mitchell sold his company for $3.1 billion in 2001. But others in the energy business got even richer during the 2000s and early 2010s. In this business, people who search out new reserves of oil or gas are called wildcatters. They are similar to modern-day treasure hunters. Thanks to the fracking boom, many wildcatters struck gold.

Two wildcatters, Aubrey McClendon and Tom Ward, were among the first to successfully combine horizontal drilling and fracking. They started Chesapeake Energy in 1989. By 2013, the company was worth $30 billion and had become the second-biggest producer of natural gas in the United States.[1]

Tom Ward, *left*, and Aubrey McClendon, *right*, aggressively bought up land over the Marcellus shale formation in Ohio and Pennsylvania.

"THE SUCCESSES OF THE ARCHITECTS OF THE SHALE ERA ARE ATTRIBUTABLE TO CREATIVITY, BRAVADO, AND THE STRONG DESIRE TO GET REALLY WEALTHY."[3]

—GREGORY ZUCKERMAN, AUTHOR OF *THE FRACKERS: THE OUTRAGEOUS INSIDE STORY OF THE NEW ENERGY REVOLUTION*

Harold Hamm, another early adopter of the new technologies, amassed a $17 billion personal fortune. He said, "In America, people lost the will to drill for oil. But I'm a little more hardheaded than other people."[2] He bought land in North Dakota over the Bakken Formation and started fracking for crude oil in 2004. But fracking for oil was not the same as fracking for gas, and at first his efforts faltered. By 2006, his company, Continental Resources, was running out of money and ready to give up, but nobody wanted the land. "Everyone had thought you couldn't get oil molecules through the shale," said Mark G. Papa of EOG Resources, another company that was trying to frack for oil in both North Dakota and Texas.[4]

Engineers at Brigham Exploration, yet another oil company working at the Bakken Formation, made a breakthrough when they drilled a very long horizontal well and then fracked it in 20 separate stages. Each fracking operation cracked the shale around only a short section of the well. Then, engineers blocked off that section and fracked again, moving down the well piece by piece. This allowed more control over the fracking process. Finally, the oil started flowing. By 2014, the Bakken was churning out nine times more oil than in 2009.

FOLLOW THE MONEY

Wherever these fracking giants went, the rush to buy up land and drill new wells created jobs and boosted the economy.

THE HALO EFFECT

Whenever one industry booms, others share in that success. The petrochemical industry, for example, turns natural gas or oil into a variety of specific chemicals that are commonly used to manufacture other products. Cheap natural gas leads to lower costs for any factory that relies on petrochemicals. In addition, each new gas or oil well requires heavy equipment, trucks, and miles of steel pipes. All of these industries benefit as well. Steel producers had been struggling, but after the boom they started building new factories to produce pipes for gas companies. Steel and glass factories also depend on fuel-guzzling furnaces to produce their products. Now, many have saved money on energy costs by using cheap natural gas in place of coal.

Judi Whittaker hoped to profit from a shale formation that lay under her New York farm. The money would have secured her farm's future.

Some landowners felt as if they had won the lottery when energy companies started paying huge sums for the right to drill under their property. In Kansas in 2012, oil companies offered as much as $1,250 per acre. The going rate had been $25 per acre the year before. "I've had to pinch myself every morning just to know I'm awake. . . . We've kind of hit the jackpot," said John Walker, a farmer in Anthony, Kansas.[5] In Louisiana, the prices were even higher—up to $30,000 per acre. Approximately two million US landowners shared in these riches.

At the height of the fracking boom in North Dakota, truck drivers made as much as $80,000 per year. These drivers carted water and other materials to and from drilling sites. The oil boom took off in 2008, the same year a major recession hit the United States. Many people who were out of work or struggling to make ends meet packed up and moved to the oil fields. Juan Ramos left a low-paying job in Florida and immediately got a temporary job on the oil fields in Williston, North Dakota, making $24 an hour—almost double his former wages.

Other businesses in North Dakota boomed, too, thanks to the influx of new workers. Restaurants started making twice as much money as before. Rent shot up for apartments, and hotels filled to capacity. At the end of 2014, Williston boasted the lowest unemployment rate in the entire country. By 2015, the

NOT IN MY BACKYARD

Some of the most vocal opponents of fracking have been the people living closest to drilling rigs, truck routes, and pipelines. They are most directly affected by any contamination or pollution from oil and gas drilling. In addition, they have to deal with noise and ugly machinery taking over their space. Often, they have no control over the decision to start drilling in their neighborhood. When community members complain about this kind of industrial development, their objections are often summarized with the phrase "Not in my backyard." In other words, these people may support shale gas as an important part of the United States' energy future, but they do not want drilling in their own neighborhood. Or they may welcome drilling only if reasonable regulations are in place to help keep them safe. For example, lawmakers could require a certain setback distance between a production site and a residential community.

MORE TO THE
STORY

WELCOME TO
NORTH DAKOTA

Once the oil started gushing in North Dakota, the rush was on. Companies including Continental Resources and EOG erected new drilling rigs at a dizzying pace. The number of rigs in the state jumped from 35 in 2009 to 173 the very next year. Each one required drillers, truck drivers, and laborers. People, mainly men, started arriving in droves from around the country, looking for work. Some would show up without a job or a place to live. Hotel rooms and apartments were scarce, so many wound up staying in "man camps," or temporary housing units. A typical worker put in 12 hours every day for two weeks and then returned home for a two-week break.

city's population had swelled to 40,000, up from 12,000 before the boom.

GROWING PAINS

This sudden growth was not all good. Some of the huge numbers of young men arriving in search of work got into trouble, and jails ran out of room as crime increased. Schools struggled to make room for growing numbers of students. They also had difficulty hiring bus drivers, cooks, and janitors, because these positions did not pay as much as the oil field jobs.

Some people who had lived in the area since before the boom felt as if their hometown had been taken away from them and transformed into something they did not recognize. "How can we allow the growth to happen, welcome people here, and at the same time remain who we are?" asked Renee Rasmussen, superintendent of a school in Bainville, Montana.[6] The town is across the state line from Williston. Despite these changes to daily life, the fracking boom greatly benefited the US economy and brought prosperity to many families at a critical time.

Loud, smelly truck traffic barrels over roads that were built for the small community of Williston, North Dakota.

Today, the rush of activity in the state has slowed. But the oil companies are there to stay, and the region will never be the same again.

TOO MUCH OF A GOOD THING

Thanks to horizontal drilling and fracking, production of natural gas in the United States skyrocketed. By 2014, the country was producing ten times more shale gas than in 2007. Over that same time period, oil production more than doubled. A basic rule of economics holds that increasing supply while demand remains the same or drops leads to decreasing prices. This is exactly what happened. The prices of both gas and oil fell to historic lows.

Dropping prices were not good for energy companies. In 2015, the number of oil rigs in North Dakota had dropped to 84 from a high of 214 in 2012. At one point, natural gas was selling for less than it cost to extract it. Companies such as Chesapeake Energy became victims of their own success. Many of these companies had borrowed billions of dollars in order to buy land and drill new wells. They had promised investors the natural gas they would find would make them rich. But the sudden oversupply of gas meant its value was not what it used to be. "We're making no money. It's all in the red," said Rex W. Tillerson of ExxonMobil in 2012.[8]

Homeowners who had leased their land to the gas companies lost out as prices dropped, too. These families typically receive royalties, payments that amount to a specific percentage of the sales of gas or oil extracted from their property. A low price for gas meant smaller royalty checks.

Many natural gas companies had to stop drilling new wells or even abandon certain locations. Towns that had swelled to support new drilling operations started to shrink again as workers left to find new jobs. Restaurants

The boom in North Dakota started winding down in 2014.

and other businesses that supported these workers lost money. Overall, however, the incredible abundance of natural gas benefited the US economy.

CHEAP ENERGY

However, low energy prices benefited homeowners and businesses. More than half of Americans use natural gas to run their stoves or heat their homes. Lower utility bills meant an average of $926 of extra spending money each year for these families. Many factories require natural gas to produce products such as fertilizer. Before the boom, many of these factories had been closing or moving overseas where the fuel was cheaper. But cheap gas meant they could continue to operate in the United States.

In fact, some experts credit the energy boom with lifting the United States out of the 2008 economic recession. The economic benefits of being able to reach previously inaccessible oil and gas resources are undeniable. Fracking and horizontal drilling made it all possible, say fracking supporters. They point to the economic facts as evidence to support continued drilling for oil and gas. They argue a successful energy industry means an economically secure future for the United States. Money, however, is not the only important thing. US citizens also want their future to be safe and clean.

Opponents around the world argue that fracking is neither safe nor clean.

CHAPTER FIVE

CLEAN ENERGY

Supporters of fracking argue that cheap natural gas helps combat climate change, while opponents say the opposite. They say cheap natural gas worsens climate change. No matter what side a person is on, the scientific evidence shows that climate change is real. It poses a huge problem for humanity as a whole. Average global temperatures are slowly warming every year. Rising temperatures mean hotter weather, more frequent and terrible storms, and other problems such as higher sea levels.

THE GOOD

Climate change is already under way. But if people switch to cleaner sources of energy, it could still be

Wind turbines are renewable sources of energy that provide electricity with very little impact on the climate.

possible to reduce the impact of climate change. Most people think of clean energy as solar panels or wind turbines. But these sources do not yet provide enough energy to take the place of fossil fuels. In addition, people still need a source of energy to fall back on when the wind is not blowing or the sun is not shining.

Natural gas is a fossil fuel, but burning it is much less harmful to the climate than burning coal or oil. Coal combustion puts approximately twice as much carbon dioxide into the air as natural gas combustion, while burning oil produces 30 percent more of the greenhouse gas.[1] Natural gas is also a more efficient fuel option. It produces much more electric energy per unit of fuel than coal.

In addition, a gas-burning power plant produces almost no sulfur dioxide, mercury, or ash pollution—all problems

COAL'S DARK SECRETS

Power plants around the world continue burning coal in order to produce electricity. Before 2015, coal provided more electricity than any other source. Now, in the United States, natural gas has pulled even with coal as the top energy source for electricity. Coal is cheap, but the process of extracting it from the ground is dangerous. The processes of mining for coal release tiny particles into the air. Regularly breathing this ash leads to disease or even death. Burning coal also pollutes the air. Overall, coal use leads to 100,000 deaths worldwide each year.[2] Coal also produces more carbon dioxide than any other energy source, making it the worst offender when it comes to climate change.

associated with coal-burning plants. In the years since the fracking boom, many coal-burning power plants have closed. This change is due to stricter environmental regulations and abundant natural gas. Power utilities have opened new natural gas plants and ramped up production at existing ones.

Many people in the oil and gas industry have pointed to the fracking boom as a great development for the future of the planet. Between 2008 and 2012, emissions of carbon dioxide in the United States fell by 13 percent.[3] Most experts attributed this drop to the fracking boom. As natural gas plants replaced coal, less carbon dioxide was released into the air.

THE BAD

Some experts, however, argued the 2008 US recession had a bigger impact on emissions levels than cheap natural gas. As the economy slumped, people used fewer energy-consuming products and services. They also traveled less, meaning the amount of carbon dioxide spewing from cars, trucks, and airplanes declined. As the economy recovers, emissions may rise again.

In addition, natural gas may be clean to burn, but it is not always clean to extract and transport. Along the way, some gas gets released into the air. According to the EPA, natural gas is composed mostly of methane, a greenhouse gas that is more than 25 times more powerful than carbon dioxide. This means that once it escapes into the atmosphere, one unit of methane will trap as much heat as 25 units of carbon dioxide.

Natural gas may leak from the well as it is extracted, from valves and fittings in pipelines, from compressor stations, or during maintenance and accidents. The compressors that help transport the gas also emit methane as exhaust from their natural-gas-powered engines. In addition, oil production sites may burn gas or vent it into the air on purpose because it is expensive to capture and transport it.

Ideally, the natural gas industry would not lose any

METHANE EMISSIONS

Leaky natural gas infrastructure may pose a danger to the climate. But when it comes to methane emissions, agriculture and landfills are just as problematic. The EPA has reported that methane emissions from agriculture are on the rise. Cows, sheep, goats, and other animals produce methane as they digest their food. Landfills, where bacteria produce methane as they break down garbage, are one of the highest producers of methane.

methane. It would capture and transport it all to be burned for energy. Though a zero percent leak rate would be impossible to achieve, much could be done to reduce existing leaks and prevent future ones.

WHAT IS THE LEAK RATE?

The amount of methane that leaks into the air matters a lot. If leak rates are too high, then natural gas could be worse for the climate than coal or oil. Research shows that leak rates must be kept below 3.2 percent for natural gas production to outperform coal in terms of climate impact.[4] According to reports by the Environmental Protection Agency (EPA), the current leak rate is 1.5 percent for the entire supply chain, from production to processing and distribution. In addition, methane emissions from the natural gas industry decreased between 1990 and 2014, even though natural gas production increased dramatically.

But other research has indicated that leaks from the natural gas industry may be higher than the EPA estimates. In 2016, the EPA admitted to this. Methane emissions come from thousands of different sites. The Environmental

Defense Fund has made a herculean effort to quantify methane emissions. They raised $18 million and funded 16 separate studies aimed at getting a better estimate of total methane emissions from the natural gas supply chain.

"We believe the leakage rates are likely higher than official estimates, but they are unlikely to be high enough to disfavor shifting from coal to natural gas," said Adam Brandt, an assistant professor of energy resources engineering at Stanford University.[5] In addition, the natural gas industry is working hard to find ways to prevent and control leaks and emissions. If it succeeds in keeping the rate low, then natural gas could indeed provide a cleaner alternative to coal and oil.

LEAKING, VENTING, AND FLARING

In its natural form, methane is invisible and odorless. So leaks may go undetected for a long time. Once the gas reaches a local distribution system, companies purposefully add a chemical to the gas that makes it smell similar to rotten eggs. This helps warn of leaks during distribution. A large gas leak from a storage facility

A health official attends a community meeting after a leak occurred in California.

operated by a distribution company in Aliso Canyon, California, made headlines in 2015.

Other leaks, however, have no such warning stench. The compressor stations that pump gas through pipelines on its way to processing plants emit a lot of methane from engines that run on natural gas. These facilities operate 24 hours per day, every day.

In addition, some oil production sites end up with natural gas they do not want. The gas often emerges from the ground along with oil, which is a much more valuable fuel. In sites that are not near natural gas pipelines, capturing, processing, and transporting that bonus gas would cost too much. So the drillers just get rid of it.

FROM THE HEADLINES

NATURAL GAS LEAK FORCES AN EVACUATION

In late 2015 and early 2016, thousands of people had to leave their homes in the Porter Ranch neighborhood of Los Angeles, California. A leak from a nearby natural gas storage facility was spewing methane and other chemicals into the air. Many residents reported headaches, dizziness, vomiting, nosebleeds, and other symptoms. "We are a family of four. My wife, our two children and myself. We all have symptoms such as headaches, nausea and an occasional nosebleed," said resident Andy Papikyan.[6] Experts said these symptoms resulted from exposure to mercaptans. This category of chemicals includes methyl mercaptan, the one that gets added to natural gas to give it a noxious odor. The governor of California, Jerry Brown, declared a state of emergency on January 6, 2016.

The leak lasted almost four months and spewed an estimated 107,000 short tons (97,100 metric tons) of methane into the air before it was permanently sealed in February 2016.[7] This equals the amount of methane gas that would be produced if an extra 500,000 cars had been driving around Los Angeles over the same time period. In response to the leak, the US government launched a task force to look into improving the safety of natural gas storage facilities.

The leak at Porter Ranch was one of the worst
natural gas leaks in US history.

There are two ways to do this. Venting lets the gas escape into the air, which adds methane to the atmosphere. Flaring burns up the gas, and releases pollutants along with a mix of greenhouse gases.

Even gas production sites may vent or flare gas during the well completion process. As drillers remove used fracking fluid, called flowback, methane comes out, too. Separating this gas from the flowback, a process known as a "green completion," requires special equipment. Using this equipment means the gas can be saved and used instead of lost. But the equipment is expensive, so in the past, many companies would vent or flare the gas instead. To address this problem, the EPA made green completions mandatory for new wells in 2012. But venting and flaring continue at old gas wells and at oil wells with no connection to natural gas pipelines.

A BRIDGE TO THE FUTURE

Researchers have suggested natural gas could serve as a

Flaring is an especially big problem at the Bakken Formation in North Dakota, an area with limited infrastructure to collect natural gas.

bridge fuel. In other words, it could supply the United States' energy demand while reducing greenhouse gas emissions until renewable energy sources are ready to take over. But some worry the eventual switch to greener energy may be difficult. The problem is that natural gas may be too cheap and easy to extract. Without demand for renewable energy technology, the renewable industry will not grow as quickly. Cheap natural gas could delay or even prevent a switch to renewable energy sources.

The fracking boom certainly had an impact on climate change. In the short term, it has helped steer people away from dirty coal and oil. But in the long term, methane leaks and a lack of incentives to invest in renewable energy could lead to big problems for the climate.

CHAPTER SIX

WATER, WATER
EVERYWHERE

Hydraulic fracturing operations consume a huge amount of water. In a typical fracking operation, workers mix water with sand and chemicals and then inject the fluid underground to break open rock formations. Much of this fluid then comes back up out of the well, carrying with it more contaminants found naturally deep underground. The drillers reuse some of the wastewater and dispose of the rest of it, typically by injecting it underground in a different location. Drillers take precautions to prevent fracking fluid or wastewater from mixing with freshwater supplies, but mistakes happen. The antifracking movement points to water usage and water contamination as two of the biggest problems associated with drilling operations.

Water usage at fracking sites is in the millions of gallons each day.

WATER COMPETITION

In Pennsylvania, fracking one well requires an average of 4.4 million gallons (16.7 million L) of water. That is equal to the amount of water that 11,000 US families use in one day, or enough to fill six Olympic-sized swimming pools. Around the country, the amount of water used to frack one well ranges widely from 2,600 gallons (9,800 L) to 9.6 million gallons (36 million L). Horizontally drilled wells suck up more water than vertical ones, because they typically extend much farther. In addition, fracking for natural gas uses more water than fracking for oil. Oil drilling relies on gel-based fluids, while gas drilling uses a slick-water formula composed of as much as 99 percent water.[1]

All this water has to come from somewhere. In certain regions of the United States,

POWER PLANT COOLING

Fracking consumes a lot of water, but so do power plants. Most power plants require vast quantities of water. These plants typically boil water to make steam. The steam turns turbines to produce electricity. In addition, the plants use water as a coolant, to absorb extra heat and prevent overheating. In fact, the electricity a typical US family uses every day consumes more water than their direct water use, including showering, cooking, and cleaning. Natural gas power plants use four times less water per unit of power generated compared with coal-burning plants. As a result, as natural gas plants replace coal plants, total water usage should decline.

Environmentalists worry energy companies will use up scarce water resources that farmers need.

such as Pennsylvania, water resources are plentiful. In other areas, though, water is scarce, and recent droughts make it scarcer. "Hydraulic fracturing is happening in places that are already facing high competition for water," said Monika Freyman, who manages the water program at Ceres, an environmental advocacy group.[2] Fracking, however, is not the biggest consumer of water. Farming consumes much more. When water is hard to come by, these industries end up competing with each other.

One possible solution to this problem is for energy companies to use water that is not fit for irrigation. For example, drillers could use salty water, or even polluted water that flows through abandoned coal mines. This would help clean up the coal mine drainage while taking less water from healthy rivers and lakes.

SHALLOW FRACKING

Most fracking happens at depths far below the water table, with thousands of feet of solid rock separating the fractures from the freshwater. But some formations that hold gas and oil occur at similar depths to aquifers or drinking water wells. In addition, there may be no solid rock layers to stop chemicals from slowly migrating through the ground and into water supplies. This is exactly what researchers suspect happened in the small town of Pavillion, Wyoming. Dominic DiGiulio of Stanford University matched chemicals from the hydraulic fracturing process to chemicals in an aquifer that provides water to the town's wells. The chemicals do not occur naturally, so fracking must have put them there. "It's perfectly legal to inject [fracking] fluids into underground drinking water resources. This may be causing widespread impacts on drinking water resources," said DiGiulio.[3]

WATER CONTAMINATION

In addition to using up water resources, oil and gas drilling operations may contaminate clean water with dangerous chemicals. When it comes to water contamination, the word *fracking* leads to misunderstandings. Oil and gas companies maintain that hydraulic fracturing does not affect water supplies. The water table is the layer of ground where drinking water comes from. Most shale formations are much deeper at 6,000 to 10,000 feet (1,800 to 3,000 m) down. Layers of

Cracks or holes in the protective casing can appear at any time in the drilling process, even after the well has been abandoned.

solid rock separate a fracked area from any aquifers, underground sources of freshwater.

But other parts of the drilling process can and do affect aquifers. Fracturing fluid or wastewater may accidentally spill or leak onto the ground while being transported or stored. Or a company may drill right through an aquifer in order to get to shale formations. Layers of cement and steel casing keep the hole separated from the water supply, but cracks or holes in this casing can allow contaminants to leak into the water.

In fact, the MIT study found that casing problems led to the majority of incidents of contamination associated with fracking operations. This kind of contamination could also happen in a nonfracked well. In a fracked well, however, the mix of chemicals added to the fracking fluid poses an additional danger if it leaks out.

DEALING WITH DIRTY WATER

Wastewater from the fracking process also poses a threat to the environment and human health. "Wastewater disposal is one of the biggest issues associated with fracking," said Avner Vengosh of Duke University.[4] The original fracking fluid mixes with brine and metals found deep underground to create a dangerous slurry that may be toxic or even radioactive. There are two types of wastewater: flowback and produced water. Immediately after fracking, the wastewater that comes back up out of the well contains a lot of fracking fluid. This is called flowback. Over time, as the fracking fluid is depleted, naturally occurring water that had been

RADIOACTIVE WASTE

Radiation is part of the natural environment. People are continually exposed to low levels of radiation from the sun and elements in rocks and soil. At higher levels, though, radiation can damage cells and cause cancer. When oil and gas wells bring up produced water from deep underground, radioactive elements often come with it. The level of radiation in wastewater varies, and in some cases may rise above acceptable levels.

trapped in the shale rock keeps on flowing. This is known as produced water, and it is typically very salty. Though produced water does not contain fracking fluid, it still may be toxic or radioactive. These contaminants come from the natural chemistry of the rock formation.

Produced water continues to flow as long as a well is active. In Oklahoma, every barrel of oil pulled from the ground comes with an average of ten barrels of produced water. "We're talking about billions of barrels, and it has to go somewhere," said Austin Holland, of the Oklahoma Geological Survey.[5]

Drillers reuse as much as 70 percent of all wastewater from fracked wells. They process it to turn it back into fracking fluid. But they must still dispose of the rest. The most common

DRILLING FOR ROAD SALT

Some towns in Pennsylvania and New York spread wastewater from drilling operations on their roads. They do not use flowback water, only produced water. The salty liquid, also called brine, melts ice in the winter and keeps dust down in the summer. It is cheaper than regular road salt because oil and gas companies need to get rid of it. But is it safe? The water typically contains high levels of toxic metals from deep underground. These contaminants could easily make their way from the road to surrounding waterways. Avner Vengosh tested samples of produced water in New York and Pennsylvania and found high levels of toxic and radioactive elements. He said, "I see it as the utmost irony that New York banned fracking but allows disposal of brine on roads."[6]

disposal method injects the toxic water back underground, into rock formations that have been deemed safe. The EPA regulates these disposal wells, which are constructed in the exact same way as a vertical oil or gas well, with layers of casing that should keep pollutants out of drinking water. Industry advocates say that failures in this system are extremely rare, but others disagree. "In 10 to 100 years we are going to find out that most of our groundwater is polluted," predicted Mario Salazar, an expert who worked on the EPA's underground injection program.[7] In addition, wastewater injection has been linked to earthquakes and sinkholes.

Another option is to clean the water, rendering it safe enough to dump into a river.

WASTEWATER PONDS

Before fracking wastewater is injected or treated, energy companies often store it in large ponds. North Dakota, Montana, and Texas store half of their wastewater this way. While sitting in these ponds, the wastewater slowly evaporates, releasing chemicals into the air and ground. In addition, birds often make a deadly mistake when they confuse the ponds for freshwater. States are starting to impose strict regulations on this kind of storage.

Most wastewater treatment plants, though, are simply not up to the task. The plants are designed to process sewage that runs down the drain in homes, businesses, and industries. But wastewater from oil and gas drilling is much more difficult to clean. In fact, the EPA recently banned regular wastewater treatment facilities from accepting fracking waste.

Even plants designed to treat fracking wastewater may not be doing a good enough job. A study by researchers at Duke University found higher than usual levels of radioactive radium as well as other contaminants downstream from a treatment facility in Pennsylvania. Plus, even if a treatment facility does manage to clean everything bad out of the wastewater, it still has to get rid of the toxic sludge that was removed.

Concerns about water contamination have fueled the antifracking movement. But industry advocates maintain the process is safe, and any incidents of contamination result from improper drilling operations or preventable accidents. As of 2016, the EPA was still reviewing the possible impacts that activities related to hydraulic fracturing had on drinking water.

CHAPTER SEVEN

MYSTERY
CHEMICALS

I n 2008, nurse Cathy Behr attended to an emergency room patient. According to Behr's report, the man had been exposed to a spill of fracturing fluids and was experiencing nausea and headaches. As a precautionary measure, the hospital evacuated the emergency room and the nurses put on protective clothing. But Behr had already been exposed. A few days later, she wound up in the emergency room with symptoms of chemical poisoning. It is not entirely clear if exposure to fracking fluid caused Behr's illness. But the fluid in question, ZetaFlow, poses an immediate and chronic health hazard, according to its documentation.

In 2013, energy company executives sat around a table and sipped fracking fluid from champagne

A Dimock, Pennsylvania, resident holds a jug of contaminated well water from her kitchen sink.

glasses. They intended to show the world that fracking chemicals can be safe. In this case, the liquid was called CleanStim, which had been developed using ingredients from the food industry, according to the manufacturer. The fluid was not meant for human consumption, but the executives said they suffered no ill effects. "I feel fine," said Michael Binnion, of Questerre Energy. "[It was] very stale-tasting."[1] Colorado governor and fracking supporter John Hickenlooper said he tried the fluid as well.

As these two stories demonstrate, fracking fluids vary wildly in their composition. Similar to chefs tweaking a recipe to suit tastes, engineers adjust the fluid to suit the composition of the rock being fractured. But manufacturers of fracking fluids often will not disclose all of the ingredients in their formulas. ZetaFlow, for example, contains two proprietary ingredients. Companies protect these formulas similar to the way Coca-Cola protects its recipes for soft drinks. If they were to publish a list of ingredients, competitors would be able to copy the recipe exactly. Then the company with the original recipe would likely lose money.

Antifracking activists argue that oil and gas companies must have something to hide. They worry fracking fluids and other pollutants from oil and gas drilling operations are poisoning the water and air and sickening animals and people. Even if fracking is performed to the highest standards, cracks in well casings, spills, or other accidents could expose the environment to these unknown chemicals.

AS SAFE AS TOOTHPASTE?

Researchers at the University of Colorado published a study on their efforts to better trace fracking chemicals and detect them in drinking water. They worked with only a small group of chemicals used in fracking, called surfactants. These chemicals, they said, were "no more toxic than common household substances."[2] Similar chemicals could be found in toothpaste, laundry detergent, and even ice cream. Some news organizations misreported the study, claiming that all fracking fluid was safe. But the researchers had looked at only a small portion of the chemical ingredients. In addition, they were not seeking to say whether the fluid was safe or not. They simply wanted to better understand its chemical composition. Their work could help match suspected cases of water contamination to specific fracking operations.

MYSTERIOUS ILLNESSES

Behr's illness is one example of an incident in which oil and gas drilling operations have caused health problems. And fracking chemicals are not the only problem. Production sites and other oil and gas facilities release airborne toxins as well. People living near oil or gas wells in Pennsylvania, Wyoming, and Colorado have reported rashes, nosebleeds, and breathing difficulties. A 2014 study looked at babies born to mothers living around natural gas wells in Colorado. The researchers found that birth defects were more common in babies whose mothers lived closest to the wells. Long-term exposure to air pollution from drilling sites may also increase the risk of cancer. In addition, workers at drilling sites risk developing silicosis from inhaling dust in the air. The dust particles damage the lungs, making it hard to breathe.

Fracking operations may also affect animals and pets. In 2012, two experts in veterinary medicine from Cornell University published a paper detailing dozens of incidents in six different states. Animals can serve as a warning system for contamination in the environment, the researchers wrote, because animals spend

XTO WASTEWATER SPILL

A wastewater storage tank cannot do its job if a valve is open, letting waste drain into the ground. This is exactly the situation that an inspector in Pennsylvania discovered in 2010. An open valve had released thousands of gallons of toxic waste over a period of two months. XTO Energy, a subsidiary of ExxonMobil, owned the tank. As a penalty for this mistake, the EPA ordered XTO to pay a $100,000 fine. In addition, the company had to spend an estimated $20 million to start recycling at least half of its wastewater, and it set up a system of alarms to alert operators to any future spills.

more time than people out in the environment, drinking the water and breathing the air. This increases their level of exposure to any toxic chemicals. Wastewater spills or leaks can be particularly dangerous, as animals may be attracted to the salty liquid.

The researchers linked wastewater spills and water contamination to deaths, illnesses, and reproductive issues in cows, horses, sheep, chickens, dogs, and other animals. They claimed the food supply was also in jeopardy. Farms in affected areas continued to grow crops, and some of the meat from affected livestock still made its way to stores.

SICK COWS

Two incidents demonstrate how drilling activities may harm animals. In one case, a farmer kept 60 of his cows in a field with access to a creek. Allegedly, drillers were dumping wastewater into this creek. Twenty-one of the cows died and sixteen did not have calves the next year. Another 36 cows living in a separate field, away from the creek, stayed healthy. Another farmer had a herd of 140 cows. Allegedly, a nearby fracking operation spilled wastewater into a pasture and a pond near the cows. Half of the animals died. In other cases, family pets and even children have become ill, typically after exposure to wastewater spills or leaks.

SECRET FORMULAS

The energy industry said the Cornell University paper did not provide scientific evidence to support the conclusion that drilling caused any health problems. The authors admitted they did not have solid evidence. One reason, they said, was that drilling companies often required people claiming contaminated water or adverse health effects to sign nondisclosure agreements. Under these agreements, the energy company would often provide some compensation to the affected family, but only if they did not speak out publicly about what had happened. Another reason was that the exact chemicals in the fracking fluid or wastewater were often unknown. So the Cornell researchers could not match chemicals found in an animal's or person's body to chemicals from nearby drilling operations.

Antifracking activists have called for drilling companies and manufacturers to publish their secret ingredients so that health complaints can be properly investigated, and so possible future health impacts can be better understood. Some companies, such as the maker of CleanStim, have worked to develop less toxic alternatives. But there is no federal law requiring disclosure of fracking fluid ingredients. In fact, the entire process of hydraulic

A jar of contaminated fracking wastewater, *right*, is compared with a visibly cleaner jar of recycled water.

fracturing avoids federal regulation, thanks to an infamous loophole.

THE HALLIBURTON LOOPHOLE

In 2005, former president George W. Bush signed the Energy Policy Act of 2005 into law. One paragraph of the document made a special exception for hydraulic fracturing. The paragraph stated that hydraulic fracturing operations would be exempt from the Underground Injection Control program of the Safe Drinking Water Act. The exception likely made its way into the law thanks to Dick Cheney, Bush's vice president. Cheney had formerly run the company Halliburton, a large oil company. Activists dubbed this the "Halliburton loophole."

The Halliburton loophole means the EPA is not allowed to regulate the hydraulic fracturing process, except when the fracking fluid contains diesel fuel. But states may regulate hydraulic fracturing, and the EPA still regulates wastewater injection.

In an attempt to remove the loophole, politicians introduced the Fracturing Responsibility and Awareness of Chemicals bill, commonly referred to as the FRAC Act, in 2009. This bill also required disclosure of fracking fluid ingredients. But the bill was not considered. It has been reintroduced twice, most recently in 2015, but the 2005 law has not changed.

AIR POLLUTION

Activists tend to focus on hydraulic fracturing fluid and its mysterious chemical composition to make fracking seem scary and dangerous. But other aspects of oil and gas drilling also impact human and animal health. As the fracking boom made drilling more widespread, health issues followed. For example, diesel or natural gas

MORE TO THE
STORY

PROTESTS AND ROADBLOCKS

Some have taken their objections to fracking to the next level. Antifracking activists have staged protests and petitioned for stricter drilling regulations or even fracking bans. They have started websites and blogs to spread what they see as the truth about fracking and have even gotten arrested. In Canada in 2013, protesters blocked a road that a shale gas company was using. When the police attempted to remove the roadblock, the situation got out of hand. The activists reportedly set police cars on fire, and the police used dogs and tear gas to subdue the violence. Forty people were arrested. In New York in 2016, protesters blocked the entrance to a natural gas storage facility.

Most of these protesters also oppose any other kind of fossil fuel development, such as the Keystone XL Pipeline or offshore drilling. They want coal, oil, and gas to stay in the ground. They believe this is the only way to protect Earth's climate. "Our leaders thought fracking would save our climate. They were wrong. Very wrong," said Bill McKibben, an author and leader of the environmentalist movement.[3]

"THE PROBLEM IS NOT NATURAL GAS OR EVEN HYDRAULIC FRACTURING ITSELF. THE PROBLEM IS THAT DANGEROUS CHEMICALS ARE BEING INJECTED INTO THE EARTH, POLLUTING OUR WATER SOURCES, WITHOUT ANY OVERSIGHT WHATSOEVER."[4]

—JARED POLIS,
US REPRESENTATIVE, COLORADO

engines power the drilling rigs, compressors, pumps, and trucks involved in drilling. All of this heavy machinery spews pollutants into the air. In addition to worsening climate change, natural gas leaks from wells and pipelines can contribute to air pollution.

Methane leaks and diesel fumes put pollutants called volatile organic compounds (VOCs) into the air. VOCs are also found in some home products, such as paint thinners and, ironically, air fresheners. When large concentrations of these pollutants build up in the air, smog forms. Smog is visible air pollution. In addition, VOCs may increase the risk of birth defects and cancer.

Using hydraulic fracturing on a new well puts more VOCs into the air than traditional drilling methods. To lessen these risks, the EPA set new air quality standards for oil and gas drilling in 2012. Companies had to start capturing excess gas using equipment known as green completions.

But even a well fracked before these regulations took effect would produce less air pollution than a coal mining operation. And thanks to fracking, coal is becoming less necessary. Still, the benefit of getting rid of dirty and dangerous coal mines does not necessarily justify the health problems and pollution associated with natural gas.

Smog wraps an area in a dusty haze that irritates the eyes, nose, and throat.

CHAPTER EIGHT

EXPLOSIONS AND
EARTHQUAKES

The health impacts of fracking and drilling may manifest slowly over a long period of time. Other drawbacks can be much more immediate and explosive. Drilling operations have resulted in earthquakes, sinkholes, and even explosions. While these disasters are not common occurrences, they call into question the safety of fracking and related technologies.

Fracking and other drilling operations produce a lot of toxic wastewater. The method typically deemed the safest for wastewater disposal involves injecting it back underground. While this approach helps prevent the pollution associated with storing wastewater

Workers do their best to follow safety guidelines, but accidents still occur.

above ground, it sometimes has another unwelcome consequence: earthquakes.

QUAKES ON THE RISE

In Prague, Oklahoma, a pair of earthquakes in November 2011 buckled part of a highway and damaged several homes. The quakes hit one day apart, the first at magnitude 5.0 and the next at 5.7.

An earthquake's magnitude reflects its strength. A magnitude over 3.0 means the quake was strong enough for people to feel. Before 2009, central and eastern states in the United States experienced an average of 24 earthquakes at 3.0 or higher each year. Between 2009 and 2014, that number climbed sharply. In 2014 alone, these states experienced 688 earthquakes. Five hundred and eighty-five of them happened in Oklahoma, a state where the average number of earthquakes per year used to be two.[1] In 2015, 907 earthquakes at magnitude 3.0 or more struck the state. Earthquakes are also on the rise in the Dallas-Fort Worth area of Texas.

STRESSED FAULT LINES

The rise in earthquakes mirrors the rise in drilling

activity due to the fracking boom. Areas with numerous

wastewater injection wells have been hardest hit.

Researchers investigating the Prague earthquakes traced

Earthquakes in Oklahoma have been on the rise since disposed wells have become more common.

the source to a wastewater disposal well. Injections of fluid into the well put pressure on fault lines, which are the places where the different plates making up Earth's crust meet. If too much stress builds up along a fault line, the plates will slip abruptly, causing an earthquake.

Stress buildup from fluid injections triggered the first earthquake. That quake shook the fault lines to cause the second, larger earthquake, scientists determined. This means the process of wastewater injection can trigger a cascade of events deep beneath the ground, leading to earthquakes powerful enough to cause damage.

DON'T BLAME FRACKING

Hydraulic fracturing involves injecting fluids deep below the ground at pressures strong enough to crack rock. In fact, the process of fracking qualifies as a very tiny, human-made earthquake. But the magnitude of these microseismic events is zero. Although fracking has been known to cause earthquakes strong enough to feel, this is very rare. Fracking typically lasts only a couple of days, and then the well starts drawing gas or oil up out of the ground. A wastewater injection site, however, blasts fluid into rock over a much longer period of time. This creates much more pressure on any nearby fault lines.

A RARE PROBLEM

Scientists have known since the 1960s that wastewater disposal wells could cause earthquakes. The fracking boom, however, increased the need for these disposal sites. In addition, many of the new fracked wells and disposal wells are close to populated areas. This makes any induced earthquakes more noticeable. Still, most disposal wells never cause a problem.

For example, North Dakota, the Gulf Coast of Texas, and Louisiana all have numerous wastewater injection wells, but very few or no earthquakes. Either the geography of these areas does not allow pressure from fluid injection to reach fault lines, or the pressure is not strong enough to induce earthquakes. Of the approximately 35,000 active wastewater disposal wells in the United States, only a few dozen have been directly linked to earthquakes strong enough to feel. In some cases, states have shut down the suspect wells or reduced the amount of fluid that can be injected. These measures typically stop the quakes.

It is not always easy to trace an earthquake to its source. The disposal well itself will not necessarily be at the center of the quake. Pressure from the well can migrate

> "THERE IS NO EVIDENCE TO SUGGEST THAT HYDRAULIC FRACTURING ITSELF IS THE CAUSE OF THE INCREASED RATE OF EARTHQUAKES."[2]
>
> —DAVID J. HAYES, DEPUTY SECRETARY, US DEPARTMENT OF THE INTERIOR

through the ground, eventually producing an earthquake as far as ten miles (16 km) away. In addition, scientists still do not know how to predict in advance which wells might produce earthquakes.

Wastewater injection can disturb the earth in other ways as well. A sinkhole occurs when water eats away at underground mineral formations, such as limestone or salt domes. This creates an empty cavity below the ground. Eventually, the roof caves in, and the sinkhole swallows up whatever was above it. In 2008, a sinkhole 900 feet (274 m) wide and 250 feet (76 m) deep opened up near a wastewater disposal site in Texas. Most likely, fluid from the disposal site ate away at an underground salt dome until the land collapsed.

BLOWOUTS AND FIREBALLS

Earthquakes and sinkholes may happen even if a drilling company is following all the laws and safety guidelines. But when a company cuts corners or when drillers make mistakes, blowouts, fires, or even explosions may result. Natural gas is highly flammable, and even at oil drilling sites, some natural gas typically comes out of the well, too.

In a blowout, oil, gas, or water bursts up from underground. The plume may ignite in a fireball. Even if a blowout does not start a fire, its explosive power can still cause damage.

Fires may start at drilling sites, processing plants, or other oil and gas facilities for many other reasons as well. If natural gas comes in contact with static electricity, a burning cigarette, or any other spark, the results could be deadly. A fracked well burst into flame in Dunkard Township, Pennsylvania, in 2014, killing one worker and injuring another. An explosion at a natural gas processing plant in Wyoming forced an evacuation of the nearby town of Opal in 2014.

The Occupational Health and Safety Administration sets standards and provides information to help prevent fires and other accidents. But even the most careful workers may slip up. In 2013, 13 workers in the oil and gas industry died in fires and explosions. That is more

DEEPWATER HORIZON

In April 2010, a gas explosion killed 11 workers on the Deepwater Horizon oil rig in the Gulf of Mexico. The explosion led to a leak that lasted three months and spilled millions of barrels of oil into the sea. Deepwater Horizon was an offshore oil rig. This type of rig drills for oil below the ocean floor and typically does not use hydraulic fracturing. But some drillers have started to secretly frack at offshore sites. The technology may be especially helpful at extreme depths.

MORE TO THE
STORY

EXPLODING WELLS

The Dunkard Township well explosion started a fire that burned for four days. Chevron, the company responsible for the accident, handed out coupons for free pizza to residents. But that was not enough to make up for the mistake. The company eventually agreed to pay $5 million to the family of the worker killed in the explosion. Similar explosions have also rocked communities in Colorado, Ohio, Texas, West Virginia, and Wyoming.

In West Virginia in 2013, two storage tanks containing flowback exploded. Five workers were treated at the hospital for burns. In Perrin, Texas, in 2014, a family suffered horrific burns after their water well exploded. They blamed nearby fracking wells and sued the drilling company. At a fracked well in Weld County, Colorado, in 2014, one worker died and two were injured when a high-pressure water valve burst. The workers had been trying to thaw a frozen pipe.

fire-related deaths than in any other private industry. In addition, the firefighters in some communities are not equipped or trained to handle the industrial fires that occur at oil and gas wells. "There is not a lot of training available yet because it's a such a new thing," said Neal Nanna, chief of the volunteer fire department in Harmony, Pennsylvania.[3]

The American Petroleum Institute, a leading prodrilling group, said the risk of fires and explosions is not high. Still, these incidents make a drilling site seem like a risky place to work. In addition, earthquakes and sinkholes lead many to wonder whether the energy industry fully understands what impact it is having when it injects fluids at high pressures into rocks far below the ground.

FROM THE HEADLINES

THE SINKHOLE THAT SWALLOWED A TOWN

In Bayou Corne, Louisiana, mining activity caused a sinkhole that forced residents out of their homes. The company responsible, Texas Brine, was not fracking for oil or gas. Instead, it was mining for brine in a salt dome. Texas Brine drilled its wells using a process called injection mining. Workers sprayed freshwater into the wells and then pumped brine to the surface. Refineries would then break the brine down into chemicals used in manufacturing.

The injection mining process hollowed out caverns in the salt dome. In 2012, one of those caverns collapsed. As swamp muck flooded the underground chambers, crude oil and natural gas bubbled up from underground and seeped into the water. The town ordered an evacuation. At first, the hole covered just approximately one acre (0.4 ha). Although Texas Brine worked to control and clean up the disaster, the sinkhole kept getting bigger. By 2015, it spanned 31 acres (13 ha), and the evacuation order had not ended. Most residents moved away, but a few stayed despite the danger.

Although hydraulic fracturing had nothing to do with this sinkhole, the accident demonstrates the riskiness of disturbing underground structures. Author and environmentalist Sandra Steingraber said, "When you keep drilling over and over and over again, whether it's into bedrock or into salt caverns, at some point you have fractured the integrity of this underground structure enough that something is in danger of collapsing."[4]

Oil is seen on top of the sinkhole in Bayou Corne, Louisiana.

THE FUTURE
OF FRACKING

The fracking boom took off in the late 2000s and then slowed in the mid-2010s as natural gas and then oil prices plummeted due to the new supply. By 2016, some gas and oil companies had failed, and many workers had lost their jobs. Yet most families and businesses have benefited greatly from the low price of energy. The United States is hungry for energy, and fracking is one of the cheapest and easiest ways to provide that energy.

TRUCKING ON NATURAL GAS

The fracking boom has already prompted many power utilities and other industries to make the switch

Switching to natural gas benefits the environment as dirty coal plants close.

to natural gas. This switch likely benefits the climate, provided that methane emissions and leaks are minimized.

If electric vehicles continue to rise in popularity, natural gas power plants could provide an even stronger benefit. The engines of gasoline and diesel-powered cars, trucks, planes, ships, and other vehicles spew a huge amount of carbon dioxide into the air. In fact, 26 percent of the United States' total greenhouse gas emissions come from transportation.[1] An electric vehicle's engine releases zero emissions when it runs. And if natural gas power plants continue to provide cheaper, cleaner, greener electricity, then charging an electric vehicle's batteries will also have very little impact on climate change.

Natural gas could also potentially replace gasoline and diesel as the fuel of choice for engines. In order to fuel an engine, the gas must be either compressed or condensed into a liquid. These two forms are known as compressed natural gas (CNG) and liquefied natural gas (LNG).

Some trucks and buses already run on these alternative fuels. President Obama visited a truck factory in North Carolina that makes vehicles that run on LNG. He said, "Trucks that you're making here at this plant run on natural gas, and that makes them quieter, it makes them better for the environment, it makes them cheaper to fill up than they would be with diesel."[2]

HOW LONG WILL IT LAST?

Before the fracking boom, many people worried that fossil fuels would run out in the near future. Then, horizontal drilling

GAS STATIONS OF THE FUTURE

LNG or CNG vehicles may run into a problem when they need to stop and fill their tanks. Natural gas stations are not nearly as plentiful as regular gas stations. Owners of electric vehicles face a similar problem finding charging stations. But this may change as companies work to build new natural gas and electric vehicle charging stations across the United States. The availability of these stations may help convince more drivers to switch to cleaner fuel sources.

and hydraulic fracturing unlocked access to previously unavailable fuels. But how much fuel? President Obama has said, "We have a supply of natural gas that can last America nearly 100 years."[3] Some scientists have said this estimate is too optimistic. One study of shale gas reserves found that these rock formations will provide a growing supply of energy through 2040. The supply will likely start to decline after that.

Fracking may keep the gas flowing for years, decades, or perhaps even a century. After that, either new

California residents protest the state government's support of fracking.

technology will provide access to more reserves of fossil fuels, or some new form of energy will take the place of oil and gas. The rate and severity of climate change will likely play an important role in determining the future of energy and of humanity as a whole.

THE DEBATE

In the future, scientists will continue to study the health, environmental, and climate impacts of fracking and drilling. Politicians and activists will also continue to debate whether the need for energy outweighs the downsides of how that energy is obtained. Some of these debates have already resulted in fracking bans. In 2011, France became the first country to ban fracking. The states of Vermont and New York have since also banned fracking.

The bans were partially because potential health impacts were not yet well understood. In states that are more supportive of oil and gas production, such as Colorado, city governments have attempted to ban fracking. The Colorado Supreme Court, however, struck down the bans in two cities. Legal battles and protests will likely continue to surround fracking.

Fracking will evolve as engineers make improvements in the machinery, fluids, and other parts of the process. Currently, the amount of water fracking requires is a cause for concern, especially in places with little water. In the future, fracking may not require any water at all. The process can work with propane gel, nitrogen, or carbon dioxide gas. All of these approaches would lower the impact on water resources while lessening the amount of toxic wastewater that would have to be cleaned or stored.

A GIFT OR A CURSE?

Despite the controversy, many consider the fracking boom to be an unexpected and important gift. The rush to buy up land and drill new wells boosted the economy and created jobs in dozens of different industries.

MORE TO THE
STORY

THE BATTLE
OVER FRACKING

Should local people be able to decide if oil and gas companies
can drill in their towns and cities? This is the legal battle that has
raged in Colorado since 2012. That year, voters in Longmont passed
a law banning fracking in their city. The next year, voters in Fort
Collins passed a similar law. The state of Colorado, however, said
these laws were illegal. Only the state itself was allowed to regulate
oil and gas drilling.

The Colorado Supreme Court decided the case in favor of
the state in 2016. In the debate building up to the decision,
emotions ran strong on both sides of the issue. "The anti-energy
activists seem to have a problem with 21st century cutting-edge
technology that helps the environment and helps society, and
that's why people don't trust these out-of-state-backed radical
environmentalists," said Jonathan Lockwood, director of a group
called Advancing Colorado.[4]

"People voted to ban fracking within city limits based upon the
constitutional right of clean water, clean air and the health of our
citizens," said Joan Peck, who co-led the 2012 petition for the ban
on fracking in Longmont.[5]

The sudden surge of natural gas and oil gave the United States a surplus of cheap energy that could lead to energy independence and better national security. Plus, natural gas seemed to be better for the environment.

But others worry this gift is tainted. Maybe natural gas is not good for the planet. Maybe the additional drilling sites and drilling methods are causing water contamination and health problems, contributing to climate change, and causing too many dangerous accidents. Maybe the risks associated with fracking are not worth the benefits.

In order to resolve these dilemmas, scientists need to continue studying fracking and its effects, and engineers need to continue developing better technology to provide safe, efficient energy. Finally, lawmakers need to take these lessons and new technologies into account when regulating oil and gas drilling.

People on both sides of the fracking debate need to find ways to listen to each other's concerns and communicate honestly and openly. The conversation also needs to go beyond fracking to consider how increased production of oil and gas will affect the future of the world and planet Earth.

ESSENTIAL
FACTS

MAJOR EVENTS

- In the late 2000s, the combination of two technologies, fracking and horizontal drilling, leads to a surge in oil and gas production in the United States. Energy companies rush to buy the rights to drill on land across the country. Some companies make billions of dollars.

- The United States will likely soon produce enough oil and gas to meet its own needs. This means the country will no longer have to buy fuel from foreign nations.

- In 2011, France bans fracking. The states of Vermont and New York followed suit in 2012 and 2015, respectively. Some towns and cities are also trying to ban fracking.

KEY PLAYERS

- George Mitchell is the first to demonstrate that fracking can successfully release natural gas from shale rock.

- Governor John Hickenlooper is a vocal supporter of fracking who opposes the efforts of several cities in Colorado to ban the controversial drilling technique.

IMPACT ON SOCIETY

The advance of new drilling technologies, including fracking, unlocked access to vast reserves of natural gas and oil in the United States. This new fuel supply boosted the economy, created jobs, lowered energy costs, and put the country on a path to energy independence. But incidents of water contamination, spills, leaks, explosions, and even earthquakes associated with fracking and other drilling operations alarmed the public and fed an antifracking movement. The fight to determine if the benefits of fracking outweigh the potential risks to people and the environment continues.

QUOTE

"After years of talking about it, we are finally poised to control our own energy future. . . . We produce more natural gas than ever before—and nearly everyone's energy bill is lower because of it."

—President Barack Obama, 2013 State of the Union address

GLOSSARY

CARBON DIOXIDE
A gas with the chemical formula of CO_2 that is released when people breathe and when fossil fuels are burned.

CASING
A pipe lining a well.

CLIMATE CHANGE
A process affecting the planet that is causing temperatures around the world to rise.

FRACKING FLUID
A liquid that is injected into a new oil or gas well in order to crack rocks.

GREENHOUSE GAS
A gas that absorbs infrared radiation and traps heat in the atmosphere.

INJECTION WELL
An underground well into which fluids are pumped for waste disposal.

METHANE

A gas with the chemical formula of CH_4 that is the main component of natural gas.

NATURAL GAS

A fossil fuel composed mostly of methane, along with a mixture of other gases such as ethane, propane, and others.

PETROLEUM

Also known as crude oil, this fossil fuel can be processed into heating oil or gasoline.

PRODUCED WATER

Water found naturally deep below the ground that comes up out of an oil or gas well along with the fuel.

PROPRIETARY

Owned by a specific company or person.

SHALE

A rock formed from condensed mud that often contains trapped natural gas.

SMOG

A combination of smoke and fog in the air.

WELL COMPLETION

The process of making an oil or gas well ready to start producing fuel.

ADDITIONAL
RESOURCES

SELECTED BIBLIOGRAPHY

Gold, Russell. *The Boom: How Fracking Ignited the American Energy Revolution and Changed the World*. New York: Simon, 2014. Print.

Prud'homme, Alex. *Hydrofracking*. New York: Oxford UP, 2014. Print.

Zuckerman, Gregory. *The Frackers: The Outrageous Inside Story of the New Billionaire Wildcatters*. New York: Portfolio Penguin, 2013. Print.

FURTHER READINGS

Bjorklund, Ruth. *The Pros and Cons of Natural Gas and Fracking*. New York: Cavendish, 2015. Print.

Farrell, Courtney. *Methane Energy*. Minneapolis, MN: Abdo, 2013. Print.

WEBSITES

To learn more about Special Reports, visit
booklinks.abdopublishing.com. These links are routinely
monitored and updated to provide the most current
information available.

FOR MORE INFORMATION

For more information on this subject, contact or visit the
following organizations:

US Energy Information Administration
1000 Independence Avenue, SW
Washington, DC 20585
202-586-8800
http://www.eia.gov
The US Department of Energy runs the Energy Information Administration
to collect unbiased energy information and share it with the general
public.

US Environmental Protection Agency
1200 Pennsylvania Avenue, NW
Washington, DC 20460
202-272-0167
http://www.epa.gov
This government agency regulates industries, including oil and gas drilling,
in order to prevent negative impacts on human health or the environment.

SOURCE NOTES

CHAPTER 1. FLAMING TAP WATER

1. "Flaming Faucets: When Fracking Goes Wrong." Online video clip. *Time*. Time, n.d. Web. 14 June 2016.

2. Ryan Tracy. "Drillers Face Methane Concern." *The Wall Street Journal*. Dow Jones & Company, Inc, 26 Sept. 2011. Web. 1 August 2016.

3. Andrew Maykuth. "PA Fines Chesapeake Energy Corp. $1.1 million for Drilling Violation." *Philly.com*. Philly.com, 18 May 2011. Web. 14 June 2016.

4. Laura Legere. "Nearly a Year After a Water Well Explosion, Dimock Twp. Residents Thirst for Gas-well Fix." *Times-Tribune*. Scranton Times-Tribune, 26 Oct. 2009. Web. 14 June 2016.

5. "Dimock, PA: 'Ground Zero' In The Fight Over Fracking." *StateImpact*. NPR, n.d. Web. 14 June 2016.

6. *FrackNation*. Dir. Phelim McAleer, Ann McElhinney, and Magdalena Segieda. Perf. Mark Ruffalo. Ann and Phelim Media, 2013. Film.

CHAPTER 2. TRAPPED IN STONE

1. Matthew Philips. "A $20 Billion Project is Poised to Transform the Natural Gas Market." *Bloomberg Businessweek*. Bloomberg, 2 Sept. 2015. Web. 14 June 2016.

2. Gregory Zuckerman. *The Frackers: The Outrageous Inside Story of the New Billionaire Wildcatters*. New York: Portfolio Penguin, 2013. Print. 18.

3. Ibid. 29.

4. Ibid. 99.

5. Russ Roberts. "Gregory Zuckerman on the Frackers and the Energy Revolution." *Library of Economics and Liberty*. Liberty Fund, 23 June 2014. Web. 14 June 2016.

CHAPTER 3. FUELING THE UNITED STATES

1. Gary Sernovitz. *The Green and the Black: The Complete Story of the Shale Revolution, The Fight Over Fracking, and the Future of Energy.* New York: Saint Martin's, 2016. Print. 5.

2. James West. "Here's What the Battle Over Iraqi Oil Means for America." *Mother Jones.* Mother Jones, 19 June 2014. Web. 14 June 2016.

3. "President Barack Obama's State of the Union Address—As Prepared for Delivery." *White House.* White House, 12 Feb. 2013. Web. 14 June 2016.

4. Matthew Philips. "A $20 Billion Project is Poised to Transform the Natural Gas Market." *Bloomberg Businessweek.* Bloomberg, 2 Sept. 2015. Web. 14 June 2016.

5. Mark J Perry. "The United States of Gas: Why the Amazing Shale Revolution Could Have Only Happened in America." *American Enterprise Institute.* American Enterprise Institute, 20 May 2014. Web. 14 June 2016.

6. "EIA Report." *US Energy Information Administration.* EIA, 27 Dec. 2005. Web. 14 June 2016.

7. Kim Ann Zimmerman. "Hurricane Katrina: Facts, Damage & Aftermath." *LiveScience.* Purch, 27 Aug. 2015. Web. 14 June 2016.

CHAPTER 4. BILLIONAIRE OR BUST

1. Christopher Helman. "Aubrey McClendon: Fracking's Cowboy Rides Again." *Forbes.* Forbes, 27 May 2015. Web. 14 June 2016.

2. Brian Gruley. "Wildcatter Finds $10 Billion Drilling in North Dakota: Energy." *Bloomberg.* Bloomberg, 19 Jan. 2012. Web. 14 June 2016.

3. Gregory Zuckerman. *The Frackers: The Outrageous Inside Story of the New Billionaire Wildcatters.* New York: Portfolio Penguin, 2013. Print.

4. Christopher Helman. "How EOG Resources Became One Of America's Great Oil Companies." *Forbes.* Forbes, 24 July 2013. Web. 14 June 2016.

5. Blake Ellis. "Farmers Hit the Jackpot in Kansas Oil Boom." *CNN Money.* Cable News Network, 25 May 2012. Web. 14 June 2016.

6. Joe Eaton. "Bakken Oil Boom Brings Growing Pains to Small Montana Town." *National Geographic.* National Geographic, 14 July 2014. Web. 14 June 2016.

7. Russell Gold. *The Boom: How Fracking Ignited the American Energy Revolution and Changed the World.* New York: Simon, 2014. Print. 46.

8. Clifford Krauss and Eric Lipton. "After the Boom in Natural Gas." *New York Times.* New York Times Company, 20 Oct. 2012. Web. 14 June 2016.

CHAPTER 5. CLEAN ENERGY

1. Donald A. Brown. "Ethical Issues with Relying on Natural Gas as a Solution to Climate Change." *Ethics and Climate.* Widener University School of Law, n.d. Web. 14 June 2016.

2. James Conca. "How Deadly Is Your Kilowatt? We Rank The Killer Energy Sources." *Forbes.* Forbes, 10 June 2012. Web. 14 June 2016.

SOURCE NOTES
CONTINUED

3. Peyton Fleming and Meg Wilcox. "New Report Shows Decline in Carbon Dioxide and Other Pollutants from US Power Plants, but State and Power Company Emissions Vary Widely." *Ceres*. Ceres, 28 May 2014. Web. 14 June 2016.

4. Ramon A. Alvarez, et. al. "Greater Focus Needed on Methane Leakage from Natural Gas Infrastructure." *PNAS*. National Academy of Sciences, 13 Feb. 2012. Web. 14 June 2016.

5. Sarah Zielinski. "Natural Gas Really Is Better Than Coal." *Smithsonian.com*. Smithsonian.com, 13 Feb. 2014. Web. 14 June 2016.

6. Daniela Gerson and Priya Krishnakumar. "My Entire Family is Sick." *Los Angeles Times*. Los Angeles Times, 7 Jan. 2016. Web. 14 June 2016.

7. Sarah Zielinski. "The Size of the California Methane Leak Isn't the Scariest Part of the Story." *Smithsonian.com*. Smithsonian.com, 26 Feb. 2016. Web. 14 June 2016.

8. Joe Romm. "IEA's 'Golden Age of Gas Scenario' Leads to More Than 6°F Warming and Out-of-Control Climate Change." *Climate Progress*. Center for American Progress Action Fund, 7 June 2011. Web. 14 June 2016.

CHAPTER 6. WATER, WATER EVERYWHERE

1. "Natural Gas from Shale: Questions and Answers." *Energy.gov*. US Department of Energy, n.d. Web. 14 June 2016.

2. Mark Jaffe. "When Drought Occurs, Fracking and Farming Collide." Denver Post. Digital First Media, 7 Feb. 2014. Web. 14 June 2016.

3. Rob Jordan. "Stanford Researchers Show Fracking's Impact to Drinking Water Sources." *Stanford News*. Stanford University, 29 Mar. 2014. Web. 14 June 2016.

4. Mark Golden. "Stanford-led Study Assesses the Environmental Costs and Benefits of Fracking." *Stanford News*. Stanford University, 12 Sept. 2014. Web. 14 June 2016.

5. Rivka Galchen. "Weather Underground." *New Yorker*. Condé Nast, 13 Apr. 2015. Web. 14 June 2016.

6. Zoë Schlanger. "Gas Industry's Solution to Toxic Wastewater: Spray it on Roads." *Newsweek*. Newsweek, 2 Mar. 2015. Web. 14 June 2016.

7. Abrahm Lustgarten. "Are Fracking Wastewater Wells Poisoning the Ground Beneath Our Feet?" *Scientific American*. Scientific American, 21 June 2012. Web. 14 June 2016.

8. Edith Honan. "UPDATE 2-NYC's Bloomberg Opposes Gas Drilling in Watershed." *Reuters*. Reuters, 25 Jan. 2010. Web. 14 June 2016.

CHAPTER 7. MYSTERY CHEMICALS

1. Matt Blake. "Bosses Toast to 'Harmless Fracking': Haliburton Executive Drinks Fluid as Part of a PR Stunt to Prove it is Safe." *Daily Mail*. Daily Mail, 1 Nov. 2013. Web. 14 June 2016.

2. "Major Class of Fracking Chemicals No More Toxic than Common Household Substances." *University of Colorado Boulder News Center*. Regents of the University of Colorado, 12 Nov. 2014. Web. 14 June 2016.

3. Bill McKibben. "Global Warming's Terrifying New Chemistry." *Nation*. Nation, 23 Mar. 2016. Web. 14 June 2016.

4. Abrahm Lustgarten. "FRAC Act—Congress Introduces Twin Bills to Control Drilling and Protect Drinking Water." *Pro Publica*. Pro Publica, 9 June 2009. Web. 14 June 2016.

CHAPTER 8. EXPLOSIONS AND EARTHQUAKES

1. Dan Satterfield. "USGS Scientists: Dramatic Increase in Oklahoma Earthquakes Is Man-Made (Updated)." *AGU*. American Geophysical Union, 11 Apr. 2012. Web. 14 June 2016.

2. David J Hayes. "Is the Recent Increase in Felt Earthquakes in the Central US Natural or Manmade?" *US Department of the Interior*. US Department of the Interior, 11 Apr. 2012. Web. 14 June 2016.

3. Ashley Smith. "New Frontier." NFPA. NFPA, 2 Mar. 2015. Web. 14 June 2016.

4. Tim Murphy. "Meet the Town That's Being Swallowed By a Sinkhole." *Mother Jones*. Mother Jones, 7 Aug. 2013. Web. 14 June 2016.

CHAPTER 9. THE FUTURE OF FRACKING

1. "Sources of Greenhouse Gas Emissions." *EPA*. EPA, n.d. Web. 14 June 2016.

2. "Remarks by the President on Energy—Mount Holly, NC." *White House*. White House.gov, 7 Mar. 2012. Web. 14 June 2016.

3. "Remarks by the President in State of the Union Address." *White House*. White House.gov, 24 Jan. 2012. Web. 14 June 2016.

4. Karen Antonacci. "Longmont Fracking Ban to Go Before Colorado Supreme Court." *Times-Call*. Digital First Media, 21 Sep. 2015. Web. 14 June 2016.

5. Kenneth Artz. "Colorado Supreme Court Considers Legality of Fracking Bans." *Heartland*. Heartland Institute, 18 Feb. 2016. Web. 14 June 2016.

INDEX

ABOUT THE
AUTHOR

Kathryn Hulick lives in Massachusetts with her husband and son, Seth. They like to hike, read, cook, visit the ocean, and play with their dog, Maya. Hulick has written many books and articles for children, about everything from outer space to video games.